DK SUPER World

JAPAN

From Mount Fuji and hot springs
to the bustling city of Tokyo,
explore the wonders of Japan

PRODUCED FOR DK BY
Editorial Caroline Wakeman Literary Agency
Design Collaborate Agency

Project Editor Amanda Eisenthal
Senior Art Editor Gilda Pacitti
Managing Editor Carine Tracanelli
Managing Art Editor Sarah Corcoran
Production Editor Siu Chan
Production Controller Rebecca Parton
Publisher Sarah Forbes
Managing Director, Learning Hilary Fine

First American Edition, 2025
Published in the United States by DK Publishing,
a division of Penguin Random House LLC
1745 Broadway, 20th Floor, New York, NY 10019

Copyright © 2025 Dorling Kindersley Limited
25 26 27 28 29 10 9 8 7 6 5 4 3 2 1
001–345867–May/2025

All rights reserved.
Without limiting the rights under the copyright reserved above, no part of this publication may be reproduced, stored in or introduced into a retrieval system, or transmitted, in any form, or by any means (electronic, mechanical, photocopying, recording, or otherwise), without the prior written permission of the copyright owner.

Published in Great Britain by Dorling Kindersley Limited

A catalog record for this book is
available from the Library of Congress.
HC ISBN: 978-0-5939-6627-3
PB ISBN: 978-0-5939-6626-6

DK books are available at special discounts when purchased in bulk for sales promotions, premiums, fund-raising, or educational use.
For details, contact: DK Publishing Special Markets,
1745 Broadway, 20th Floor, New York, NY 10019
SpecialSales@dk.com

Printed and bound in China

www.dk.com

This book was made with Forest Stewardship Council™ certified paper – one small step in DK's commitment to a sustainable future. Learn more at www.dk.com/uk/information/sustainability

CONTENTS

MAP — 4
Japan

FACT FILE — 6
All About Japan

TERRAINS — 8
Volcanoes, Forests, and Coasts

LANDMARKS — 10
Mount Fuji

FLORA AND FAUNA — 12
Snow Monkeys to Spider Crabs

CULTURE — 18
Customs, Pop Culture, and Sports

RELIGION — 22
Shinto and Buddhism

NATIONAL HOLIDAYS AND FESTIVALS — 24
Celebrations

FOOD AND DRINK — 26
Rice, Noodles, and More!

RECIPE — 28
Bento Box

HOME, WORK, AND SCHOOL — 30
In the City and the Country

SCHOOL DAY DIARY — 32
Hinata's Day

HISTORY — 36
From Ancient Times to Today

THE ONE-INCH BOY — 38

VOCABULARY BUILDER — 42
Describing Forests

GLOSSARY — 44

INDEX — 46

Words in **bold** are explained in the glossary on page 44.

JAPAN

Japan is an **archipelago** in East Asia. It is made up of thousands of islands—more than 14,000!— but most people live on the five main islands: Hokkaido, Honshu, Shikoku, Kyushu, and Okinawa. Japan is known for its food, strong sense of culture, and incredible natural landscapes.

FASCINATING FACT!

To get between islands, people use cars, trains, and ferries. The longest bridge is the Kurushima Kaikyō Bridge, connecting the island of Ōshima to Shikoku. It is 13,173 feet (4,015 m) long!

FACT FILE

ALL ABOUT JAPAN

Cherry blossom

Nisshoki

- 🚩 Flag: Nisshoki
- 📍 Capital city: Tokyo
- 👤 Population: Approx. 124 million
- 💬 Official language: Japanese
- 💴 Currency: Japanese Yen ¥
- 🌸 National flower: Cherry blossom
- 🐾 National animal: Green pheasant
- 🐟 National fish: Koi
- 🎵 National anthem: Kimigayo ("His Imperial Majesty's Reign")
- 👕 National dress: Kimono
- ⭐ Major export: Vehicles

 FASCINATING FACT!

Japanese people love vending machines! You can find t-shirts in a can, freshly made pizzas, and even edible bug snacks like grasshoppers, roasted crickets, and diving beetles.

Capital city

Tokyo is the most densely populated city in the world, with more than 37 million people. It was built up from a small fishing village that was first called Edo.

National dress

A kimono is a type of traditional robe that wraps around the waist, worn by all genders. Kimonos are usually worn for special occasions and formal events.

Getting around

Japan is home to the bullet train, a high-speed railway network that has some of the fastest trains on Earth. The trains can travel around 200 miles (320 km) per hour.

FIND OUT!

The word for Japan in Japanese is *Nippon*, which means "the land of the rising Sun." What is the name of your country? Does it have a special meaning?

TERRAINS

VOLCANOES, FORESTS, AND COASTS

Japan has extremely diverse landscapes, from the **subtropical** beaches on the southern island of Okinawa, to the snowy **mountains** of Hokkaido, to the mystical ancient forests of Kyushu.

Hot stuff
The islands of Japan are in the Ring of Fire, which is an area in the Pacific Ocean where four **tectonic plates** meet under the Earth's crust. That means there is a lot of volcanic activity. It is estimated that Japan has more than 100 **active volcanoes**!

Sakurajima

Hot springs
Japan's volcanic activity also results in hot springs! All over Japan, there are steaming hot **geothermal** pools of water called *onsen*. Both animals and humans enjoy bathing in them!

Wild places

More than 60 percent of Japan is uninhabited by people. That's because it's covered in **mountains** and ancient forests. In fact, 90 percent of the people live in just 10 percent of the land. Forests tend to be luscious and full of wildlife.

Subtropical beaches

The islands in the south are subtropical. They have hot summers and milder winters, as well as a lot of rain. Okinawa in particular is known for its beautiful beaches. The water around the main Okinawa island is always 68–86°F (20–30°C)—perfect for snorkeling.

FIND OUT!

Japan faces South Korea on the west and a wide expanse of the Pacific Ocean on the east. Do you know what continent it is part of?

Answer: Asia

Cold climates

Further north, the land becomes much more rugged and experiences heavy snowfall in the winter. The mountains of Hokkaido get an average of 49 feet (15 m) of snow per year. One of the favorite hobbies there is skiing.

 LANDMARKS

MOUNT FUJI

At a massive 12,389 feet (3,776 m) tall, Mount Fuji is the highest mountain in Japan. In fact, Mount Fuji is so tall, it can be seen all the way from Tokyo, 60 miles (100 km) away.

Volcanic activity

Mount Fuji is still an active volcano that erupts about once every 500 years. The last eruption was in 1707 and was triggered by an earthquake of a whopping 8.4 magnitude. That's a big earthquake! The **ash** cloud was so huge, it even reached Tokyo.

 FASCINATING FACT!

Until around 1868, women were forbidden to climb Mount Fuji. It was believed they would anger the goddess of Mount Fuji, Konohanasakuya-hime.

Inside a volcano

Mount Fuji is a **stratovolcano**, which means it is made up of layers and layers of **lava** from past eruptions. That's what gives Mount Fuji its iconic cone shape.

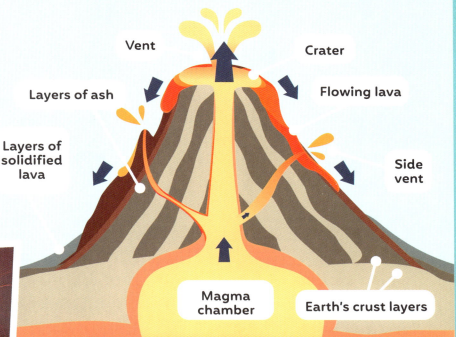

Exploding rock

Stratovolcanoes have sticky, viscous **magma** that traps a lot of gas. The buildup of pressure from this gas results in huge explosive eruptions! They can even spurt out flying lumps of rock called volcano bombs.

The Great Wave

Artists and poets have always been inspired by Mount Fuji. There are many beautiful works of art depicting it, including the world-famous print, *The Great Wave off Kanagawa.*

FIND OUT!

The country of Japan is made up of hundreds of islands. Can you find out which island Mount Fuji is on?

Answer: Honshu

FLORA AND FAUNA

SNOW MONKEYS TO SPIDER CRABS

The incredible diversity of terrain in Japan means that a huge variety of animal and plant life can flourish. Ocean life also thrives due to the mixing of warmer water from the **Tsushima current** with the colder **Sea of Japan**.

FOREST FRIENDS

Japanese macaque
These critters are often called snow monkeys because they love to use the natural hot springs called *onsen* to keep warm in the winter snow. Macaques live in forests in troops of about 20–30 individuals.

FASCINATING FACT

Snow monkeys are the only creatures besides humans and raccoons known to wash their food before eating.

Green pheasant
The *kiji* is the national bird of Japan. The males are bright green with blue and red heads, while the females are brown for camouflage. Green pheasants can detect movements in the earth too small for humans to feel and will call out if they sense earthquakes.

Raccoon dog
Also called *tanuki*, these raccoon-like mammals are part of the canidae family, and are most closely related to the fox. Unlike most **canids**, they can climb trees to forage for berries and nuts. They are **omnivores** so they also eat small mammals, frogs, and even poisonous toads!

Japanese serow
These are stocky long-haired, goat-like mammals **endemic** to the forests of Japan. Serows were once almost hunted to extinction, but **conservation** efforts have been so successful they are now classed as animals of "least concern" on the **endangered** list.

BRED ANIMALS AND INVASIVE SPECIES

Hunting hound
Shiba Inu were **selectively bred** as hunting dogs about 2,300 years ago. They are now prized for their intelligence and their thick orange fur, though not for their stubbornness!

Invader!
Snapping turtles were brought to Japan from the Americas as exotic pets in the 1960s. They are classified as an **invasive species** because they wreak havoc on their habitats, munching through fish populations and disturbing **ecosystems**.

Decorative fish
Koi carp might be the national fish of Japan, but they were actually only brought to Japan about 2,000 years ago. They have since been selectively bred to come in all shapes, sizes, and colors.

AQUATIC ANIMALS

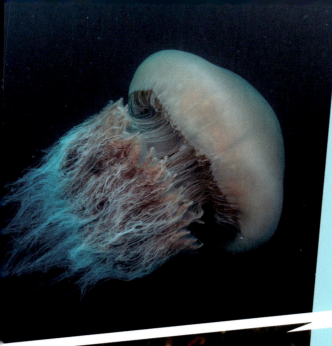

Nomura's jellyfish
These jellyfish weigh up to 440 pounds (200 kg). They are named after Kan'ichi Nomura, who discovered this species in 1921. Nomura's jellyfish sometimes appear in "blooms" of thousands and can get caught up by fishing fleets around Japan.

Giant squid
Giant squid really are giant! They measure up to 43 feet (about 13 m) and have the biggest eyes of any known animal. They feed by catching fish with their tentacles and reeling them into their beaks. Their main predators are sperm whales.

Spider crab
Japanese spider crabs may look alien, but **fossils** suggest they have been on Earth for millions of years. They are the largest **crustacean** in the world, growing up to around 12.5 feet (4 m).

| Human
5.6 feet (1.7 m) | Nomura's jellyfish
6.6 feet (2 m) | Japanese spider crab
12 feet (3.7 m) | Giant squid
42.6 feet (13 m) |

BOTANICAL BEAUTIES

Sakura
Cherry blossoms are so important to Japanese culture that festivals are held every year when the flowers start to bloom. The soft pink flowers are known as *sakura*.

Bamboo
Giant timber bamboo grows at an astonishing rate, as fast as 36 inches (91 cm) in a single day!

Lotus
Lotus flowers are an important symbol in **Buddhism**, representing purity and enlightenment. Their roots are also delicious.

Yakusugi
Ancient Japanese cedar (*yakusugi*) trees can live thousands of years. Yakushima island is a magical wonderland of *yakusugi* trees, including the tree named *Jomon Sugi*, estimated to be between 2,000 and 7,000 years old.

ENDANGERED SPECIES

Even though so much of Japan is wild, humans still have a big impact on the environment.

Overfishing
Bluefin tuna numbers were reduced to as low as 4 percent of their original population due to the massive fishing **industry** in Japan. Fishing practices also damage coral reefs and other underwater ecosystems.

Habitat loss
The Okinawa rail is a small flightless bird only found in the Yanbaru forests on the island of Okinawa. It is one of the most endangered species in Japan. It is impacted by habitat loss due to farming and **forestry**, as well as by the introduction of predators like cats.

Pollution
The Japanese crested ibis nearly went **extinct** because there was so much **pollution** from Japan's cities throughout the 20th century. Conservation and **sustainability** efforts have helped species like these recover in recent years.

CULTURE

CUSTOMS, POP CULTURE, AND SPORTS

Japan has a strong and unique culture that emphasizes honor and politeness, as well as fun! Japan has given the world iconic pop culture staples like video games and anime. It has also embraced culture from overseas, as seen in its love of baseball.

Being polite
Manners are very important in Japan. The term *-san* can be added to the end of a name to show respect. Before they tuck into their meal, Japanese people will often say *Itadakimasu!* meaning "I humbly receive"—or "thank you for the food!"

CUSTOMS

Luck
Maneki-neko is the name for the cat ornament with a raised paw that you're likely to see around Japan. It is said to bring luck and wealth. Other symbols of luck include cranes, *tanuki*, and the number seven.

Origami
Origami is the ancient art of paper folding, practiced for thousands of years. It is said that if you fold 1,000 paper cranes, you will be granted a wish. Origami is so important in Japanese culture it is even taught in kindergarten.

Names and titles
In Japan, the family name (or surname) comes before the first name.

Tanaka Hinata (Full name) **Hinata** (First name) **Tanaka** (Family name)

You can show respect or friendship using titles at the end of a name:
- *san*: formal, such as for a teacher or neighbor. *Mitsuo-san*
- *chan*: friendly and mostly for a girl, like a sister, friend, or grandma. *Hinata-chan*
- *kun*: friendly and mostly for a boy, like a brother, friend, or grandpa. *Ren-kun*

POP CULTURE

Anime
Anime is a Japanese style of cartoon, and it's popular in much of the rest of the world too. It tends to be colorful and fast-paced and is enjoyed by kids and adults alike. Anime is sometimes based on comic books called manga that are read from back to front.

Kawaii
The term *kawaii* refers to anything cute, and it's a huge **cultural phenomenon** in Japan. Clothes, video game characters, advertisements, and even trains and planes have adopted the *kawaii* style. It typically has bright colors, huge eyes, fluffy characters, and rounded shapes.

Gaming
Japan loves video games! Some of the first game consoles came from Japan, and Tokyo is the headquarters for many of the big game companies. Arcades are also a major pastime. In Tokyo, you can find arcade centers that are six floors high!

SPORTS

Sumo

Japan's oldest sport is sumo wrestling: two wrestlers try to force each other out of a ring marked on the floor, and the first to touch the ground outside the ring loses. Sumo wrestlers often weigh around 330 pounds (150 kg)! That makes it harder to be pushed around.

Baseball

Baseball is a favorite sport in Japan. There are 12 professional teams in two main leagues: Central and Pacific. Many people play with friends in their spare time.

Martial arts

Judo and karate are popular martial arts in Japan. The name "Judo" translates as "the gentle way." The aim is to use your opponent's strength against them with grappling and throwing moves. Karate means "empty hand." Karate focuses on striking with kicks and punches, as well as blocking.

FIND OUT!

What is the most popular sport in your country?

Judo fighters

RELIGION

SHINTO AND BUDDHISM

The two main religions in Japan are **Shinto** and Buddhism, and many people follow both. Shinto is the oldest religion in Japan, while Buddhism was introduced around the 6th century.

Shrines
Followers of Shinto believe that people are born good, and that badness comes from evil spirits. People ward away evil spirits with prayer and purification rituals, and many go to **shrines** to perform these rituals.

One of the most important *kami* is *Amaterasu*, the spirit of the Sun.

The Spirits of Shinto
Followers of Shinto worship *kami*. These are spirits which often take the form of elements of nature, such as animals, mountains, waterfalls, and forests. Tree *kami*, for example, are called *kodama*. Shinto promotes harmony between people and the natural world.

You can recognize a Shinto shrine by its iconic gates, called *torii*.

Temples

Japan has thousands of Buddhist temples where people go to worship, chant, and meditate. The oldest temple is Sensō-ji, built in 645 CE!

Many Buddhists who live in or visit temples follow a plant-based diet called *shojin ryori*. This is intended to avoid harming any living thing.

The way of the Buddha

The founder of Buddhism was Siddhartha, a prince who left his royal life in search of enlightenment—a state of full understanding and spiritual awakening. Buddhists practice **meditation** to help achieve enlightenment.

Other religions

Europeans tried to bring Christianity to Japan in the 1500s, but it didn't really stick. These days, only a tiny percentage of the population consider themselves Christian. Immigrant communities have also introduced other religions, like Hinduism, Islam, Judaism, and Sikhism.

NATIONAL HOLIDAYS AND FESTIVALS

CELEBRATIONS

kadomatsu

otoshidama

Japan has 16 public holidays each year, and even more festivals. Celebrations are often full of color, food, and fun.

PUBLIC HOLIDAYS

New Year's Day
On January 1, people flock to temples and shrines to pray for a good year ahead. Children receive *otoshidama*—money from relatives in decorative envelopes—and bamboo *kadomatsu* decorations are put out to welcome *kami* spirits.

Coming of Age Day
On the second Monday of January, people celebrate teenagers becoming adults. Traditionally, girls wear a kimono called a *furisode* and boys wear a pair of wide pants called *hakama*.

Children's Day
May 5 celebrates children. *Koinobori* banners in the shape of koi are flown: black (*ma-goi*) for the father, red (*hi-goi*) for the mother, and differently colored banners for each child in the family.

FESTIVALS

Snow festival
The Sapporo Snow Festival in Hokkaido is a week-long event in February. It's an international snow sculpture competition, with activities like ice mazes and snow slides, live performances, and food and drink.

Omizutori
In March, the Buddhist festival Omizutori is held, signifying the cleansing of sins and the start of spring. Monks with huge torches spray fiery sparks across the crowds.

Cherry blossom festival
Between March and May across the main islands, cherry blossom festivals are held to celebrate the blooming of the *sakura* cherry blossom flowers.

FOOD AND DRINK

RICE, NOODLES, AND MORE!

Japan is famous for its food. The capital city of Tokyo has more restaurants per person than anywhere else in the world. The Japanese diet contains lots of fish, rice, and vegetables, and is typically nutritious and low in fat.

maki

urakami

nigiri

Sushi
This classic Japanese dish is made from sticky rice with fish or vegetables. It is often formed into bitesized shapes.

Ramen
This is a noodle soup made with broth and noodles topped with meats and vegetables. Traditional toppings include roast meats, bamboo shoots (*menma*), seaweed (*nori*), a swirly pressed fish cake (*kamaboko*), and boiled eggs.

FASCINATING FACT!

In Japan, it is not rude to slurp your noodles. In fact, slurping is said to improve the flavor!

Green tea
This caffeinated drink is the most-consumed beverage in Japan. It can be served hot or cold, and there are traditional tea ceremonies that can last for hours.

Curry rice
This unofficial national dish of Japan is simply curry with vegetables or meat served with rice. The curry is often made from solid blocks of spices and stocks melted in hot water.

Bubble tea
This colorful cold tea drink is flavored with tapioca bubbles, sometimes made with fruit. It is so loved in Japan that there is a slang term for drinking bubble tea: *tapiru*.

Sandwiches
The *tomago sando* is a popular egg sandwich found in convenience stores. It is made of mashed boiled eggs, sometimes with mayonnaise, spread between two thick slices of soft milk bread.

Here are some other popular foods:

Mochi
rice cake traditionally lled with a sweet red ean paste.

Bento box
A meal in a box often taken for a packed lunch.

Katsu curry
Breaded cutlets of meat or vegetables in a curry sauce.

Tempura vegetables
Vegetables fried in a crispy batter.

RECIPE

BENTO BOX

A bento box is like a Japanese lunch box with compartments for different foods, like rice or noodles, vegetables, and fruit. Create your own bento box with these fun recipes!

STICKY SEASONED SUSHI RICE

Ingredients
- 1 cup (200 g) of short grain sushi rice
- 1 ¼ cups (600 ml) of water
- 5 tbsp. (75 ml) of rice vinegar
- 1 ½ tbsp. (20 g) of sugar
- ½ tsp. of salt

This makes 3 servings of rice.

Method
1. Wash the rice thoroughly. Let it soak in cold water for 15 minutes, then drain it.
2. In a large pot, add the water and the rice and bring it all to boil—ask an adult to help. Once it is boiling, cover the pan with a lid and turn it to a low heat.
3. Let it cook for about 12 minutes or until all the water is gone.
4. Leave the lid on but take the pan off the heat. Leave it to steam for 15 minutes.
5. In a bowl, stir the salt and sugar into the rice vinegar until it is all dissolved.
6. While the rice is still warm, pour the vinegar mix onto it. With a large spoon or spatula, fold the rice over several times to mix it in.
7. Spoon the rice into the bento box.

FRUIT SANDO

Ingredients
- Handful of your favorite fruit
- ½ cup (125 ml) of whipping cream
- 1 tbsp. (12.5 g) of sugar
- 2 slices of soft white bread (crusts removed)

This makes 1 serving.

Method
1. Cut your favorite fruit into bitesize chunks.
2. Whip up the cream and sugar until it thickens.
3. Spread the cream onto one slice of bread and place the fruit on top. Fill in any gaps with cream.
4. Close the sandwich and cut it diagonally.
5. Then place in your bento box.

RAINBOW VEGETABLES

1. Get some of your favorite vegetables. Make them colorful! Some good ones to use are:
   a. Broccoli
   b. Cherry tomatoes
   c. Edamame beans
   d. Bell peppers
   e. Snap peas
2. Cut them into strips and bitesized pieces.
3. Arrange them in your bento box.

SAUCE IDEAS!

Try drizzling one of these over your rice to give it some extra taste:
- sticky teriyaki
- savory shoyu
- citrusy ponzu

HOME, WORK, AND SCHOOL

IN THE CITY AND THE COUNTRY

In city centers, people tend to live in apartment blocks. Further out in suburbs, towns, villages, and the countryside, more people live in houses.

Japanese houses
Traditional Japanese homes are raised up on stilts and have sliding doors made of wood and paper. A dining area is often laid with bouncy *tatami* mats. Families sit on the floor or cushions to eat at a low table. It is customary to take your shoes off before entering someone's home, and people tend to wear house slippers inside.

Traditional Japanese house

Going to school

In Japan, children can leave school at 15, but many choose to go to high school. Students learn math, science, art, physical education, Japanese, foreign languages, and social studies. Moral education class teaches children how to be good people and citizens. In rural areas, schools might only have about 10 students!

Elementary:
6–12 years old

Junior high:
12–15 years old

School stages

High:
15–18 years old

FASCINATING FACT!

The Japanese alphabet is made up of three different systems of writing: *hiragana*, *katakana*, and *kanji*. In school, children learn each one at different stages.

Japan in *kanji*

Working in the city

Japan is known for its technology: cars, electronics, IT, medical technologies, even robotics! In many regions, particularly cities, these are the main industries.

Working outdoors

Japan has one of the largest fishing fleets in the world and catches more than 3 million tons of fish a year. Its biggest **export** is scallops! The main crop is rice, grown by farmers in paddies, which are fields half submerged in water.

SCHOOL DAY DIARY

HINATA'S DAY

Name: Tanaka Hinata
Age: 10
Lives: Just outside of Nara
Family: Mom, Dad, brother (Tadashi)

Ohayō! My name is Hinata! This is my school day in 5th grade! I get up a bit late and have to put my clothes on in a hurry. I don't have to wear a uniform, but my older brother is in Junior High and he wears a blazer called a *gakuran*.

My parents made me my favorite breakfast: miso soup with egg and tofu.

I fit in my piano practice before it's time to leave. Oh! I forgot to pack my books! (Too many books)

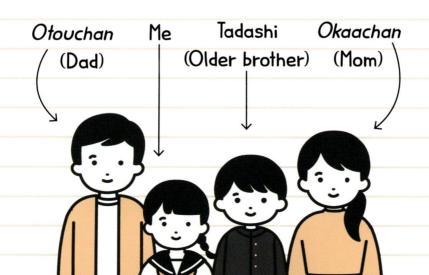

Otouchan (Dad)   Me   Tadashi (Older brother)   *Okaachan* (Mom)

My dad walks me to the corner to meet my classmates. I walk to school with my classmates every day, even in the snow.

We get to school at around 8.20 and change into our inside shoes (*uwabaki*) and go to homeroom. My best friend Ren lives on the other side of town and has a different walking group.

Before classes, we have our *toban*. Today, Mei takes attendance, then Ren and I clean the desks. Other kids sweep floors or clean out the rabbits.

Toban: School duties, such as cleaning, taking attendance, and serving lunch.

Then it's time for morning classes. Ren and I and our homeroom have:

Math
Science
Recess (soccer time!)
Moral education (*doutoku*)
Japanese reading and writing

Japanese is my favorite. We're doing **calligraphy** today. I love to use the brush. This is the *kanji* for "open." It's easy to remember because it looks like two hands opening a gate!

開

Kanji: Japanese picture characters that represent whole words.

Lunch time (*kyushoku*)! I'm not on lunch *toban* today and neither is Ren, but our friends Iru and Yuki are. We go to the lunchroom and they serve us our food, then we take it back to home room. This is what we have. *Itadakimasu!*

> *Itadakimasu*: I will humbly receive.
> In Japan, people say this phrase before a meal to express gratitude and appreciation for the food received.

When we're done, Yuki and Iru come to clear our trays, then Ren and I get to go outside for recess. We play *janken* and Ren loses, so he has to go in goal this time.

> *Janken*: A game of Rock, Paper, Scissors.

After recess we have gym class. We warm up on the *tobibako* and then play volleyball. We get changed, and it's time for cleaning, then home time.

> *Tobibako*: Jumping box

Lunch (*kyushoku*)

I usually go home with my walking group, but Ren and I just started going to Tea Ceremony Club. I wanted to learn the traditional way to brew and pour tea. Since we're new, we mostly watch the older students and learn from them, and then we get some nice hot tea.

tea whisk (*chasen*)

tea container for the powdered green tea (*natsume*)

kettle (*kama*)

tea bowl (*chawan*)

tea scoop (*chashaku*)

Time to go home! My dad comes to pick me up. When we get in, I can smell Mom and Tadashi cooking curry rice for dinner (yum!), so I do my *kanji* homework in my workbook so I'm all ready. We sit on the *tatami* mats to eat–*itadakimasu!*–and then afterwards I play some video games with Tadashi before finishing my piano practice.

Before bed, I prepare my things for tomorrow. I sharpen my pencils and pack my books so I don't forget like I did this morning. Then it's bedtime! Goodnight (*Oyasumi*)!

HISTORY

FROM ANCIENT TIMES TO TODAY

People first came to Japan from mainland Asia 33,000 years ago by walking over land bridges. Early societies were mainly fishers and hunter-gatherers, until the Yayoi people arrived around 350 BCE.
They used tools, made things from bronze and iron, and even grew rice in paddy fields. At this time, emperors ruled the land.

FASCINATING FACT!

Ninjas were real! The emperors and shoguns used ninjas as spies and assassins. The art of ninja fighting is called *ninjutsu*.

Shoguns

Around 1185, military leaders called shoguns took control by force. They united Japan into one nation, took power, and enforced a **feudal system**. Powerful people were protected by samurai warriors: master swordsmen who wore ornate sets of armor.

Samurai

Isolation

In 1543, traders and Christian **missionaries** arrived from Europe. Around 1633, Japan's leaders kicked them out and began an era of *sakoku* (isolation), closing their borders for 200 years. This lasted until the shogun were overthrown by supporters of Emperor Meiji.

Emperors strike back

In 1868, emperors returned to power and Japan started an era of modernization known as the Meiji Restoration. Contact with Europeans and Americans was allowed at last, foreign technology was introduced, and many roads, houses, businesses, and railroads were built.

Emperor Meiji

World wars

When World War I broke out in 1914, Japan fought with the Allies—Britain, France, Russia, and the USA. But during World War II (1939–1945), Japan sided with the German army against the Allies.

Japan today

Japan has had enormous economic growth since World War II and is now one of the largest economies in the world. It is a **democracy**, so emperors still exist, but they no longer rule. Instead, Japan is led by a prime minister.

VOCABULARY BUILDER

DESCRIBING FORESTS

Forest bathing (*shinrin-yoku*) is the ancient Japanese practice of relaxing in nature. The idea is to breathe in the fresh air, observe nature, and enjoy the forest environment in peace. Read this description of a relaxing visit to the Aokigahara forest on the side of Mount Fuji.

Aokigahara forest

The forest is like a sea of trees, with dense leaves above and springy moss and knotted roots below. The first thing I notice is that it is so quiet. The ground is made of volcanic rock that's full of holes, and the holes dampen sounds. That's what makes it so peaceful.

The forest has lots of wildlife, like boars that snuffle in the dirt and plow for food, and sleek Japanese weasels that dart along branches and into burrows. There are even Asian black bears, with a white crescent moon shape on their chests. They lumber on the ground and clamber up trees.

I can hear a pygmy woodpecker tapping at a tree nearby. I'm sure I saw something moving in the ferns, too.

Things in the forest
animals, birds, branches, canopy, dirt, ferns, leaves, moss, roots, soil, trees, trunks, volcanic rock, wildlife

Descriptive words
calm, close, dense, heavy, knotted, mysterious, peaceful, private, quiet, restful, shady, springy, warm

Asian black bear

Japanese weasel

Actions words
clamber, climb, dart, lumber, plow, scamper, scramble, slink, snuffle, tap, trot

Imagine you are walking gently through a forest near you. Write a description of your walk.
- What can you see?
- What can you hear?
- What animals do you encounter?

Use the words in the vocabulary boxes above to help you.

GLOSSARY

Active volcano A volcano that has erupted in the last 10,000 years or that shows signs that it could erupt in future.

Archipelago A group or chain of islands.

Ash A mixture of rock fragments, minerals, and glass that is expelled from a volcanic eruption.

Buddhism A religion based on the spiritual teachings of the Buddha that promotes meditation and enlightenment.

Calligraphy The art of decorative writing with a brush or special pen.

Canid An animal from the dog family, such as a wolf, dog, or fox.

Conservation The preservation and protection of animals, habitats, and ecosystems.

Crustacean An aquatic creature without a spine that usually has a hard shell, such as a lobster or shrimp.

Cultural phenomenon A trend or interest that spreads widely within a society or group of people.

Democracy A form of government in which the people in power are elected by the general population.

Ecosystem A community of plants, animals, and other environmental factors that exist together with relationships and interactions that affect each other.

Endangered At risk of extinction.

Endemic Native to a specific area or country and mainly or only found in that area or country.

Export Something sold from one country or region to another country or region.

Extinct Having died out and no longer existing.

Feudal system A society that is organized by rank, where higher ranked people have power and land and lower ranked people work for them.

Forestry Wood industry that sometimes involves cutting down trees and selling them.

Fossil An organism from past geological eras that has been preserved, often found in rock.

Geothermal Heated by the Earth.

Humid Both hot and damp at the same time.

Industry A particular area or type of business. For example, the automobile industry refers to the manufacture and sale of vehicles.

Invasive species A species that is non-native to an area but that has been introduced to and colonized that area. They are usually harmful to their environments.

Lava Very hot liquid or semiliquid rock that has emerged onto the Earth's surface, usually as the result of a volcanic eruption.

Magma Very hot liquid or semiliquid rock found under the Earth's surface.

Meditation The practice of clearing your mind or controlling your focus to achieve a state of calm.

Missionary A religious person sent to a foreign area to raise awareness of their faith or convert others to their religion.

Mountain A high, steep landform.

Omnivores Animals that eat both meat and vegetation.

Pollution Substances and materials that are harmful or poisonous to an environment.

Population The people or organisms who live in a certain area. It can also mean the number of people or animals that live in a certain area.

Sea of Japan The sea between Japan and the mainland countries of Korea and Russia.

Selectively bred The process of breeding animals (or plants) with particular characteristics, such as long legs or orange fur, to produce offspring with those characteristics.

Shinto A Japanese religion that focuses on honoring ancestors and spirits of nature and celebrates the wonders of the natural world.

Shrine A holy place where people worship, often indicated by a landmark or collection of items.

Stratovolcano A type of volcano formed when layers of lava build up over multiple eruptions.

Subtropical Regions close to the tropics (the area around the equator), usually with mild-to-hot weather.

Sustainability The practice of conserving and managing natural areas and resources so that they can exist in future generations.

Tectonic plates Large solid slabs of rock beneath the Earth's surface which lay over a layer of hot magma.

Tsushima current Ocean current around the west coast of Japan with warmer water than the Sea of Japan.

Volcano A vent in the Earth's crust where lava, hot ash, and gases erupt from or have erupted from in the past.

INDEX

A
alphabet, Japanese 31, 33
anime 20
Aokigahara forest 42
archipelago 4
　see also islands
Asian black bear 42, 43

B
bamboo 16, 24
baseball 21
bento 27, 28–29
birds 6, 13, 17
bluefin tuna 17
boars 42
bubble tea 27
Buddhism 16, 22–23, 25

C
cedar trees 16
cherry blossoms 6, 16, 25
Children's Day 24
climate 9
clothing 6, 7, 24, 32
Coming of Age Day 24
crested ibis 17
culture 18–21
　see also customs
curry rice 27
customs 10, 18–19, 26, 30

D
dogs 13, 14
drinks 27

E
earthquakes 10, 13
Edo 7
education 31, 32–35
emperors 36, 37
endangered species 13, 17
enlightenment 16, 23
environment, human impact on 17

F
fact file 6–7
farming 17, 31, 36
fauna 12–15, 17, 42–43
festivals 16, 24–25
feudal system 37
fishing 15, 17, 31, 36
flora 16, 42–43
food 23, 26–29, 32
forests 8, 12–13, 16, 17, 22, 42–43

G
gaming 20
giant squid 15
government 37
green pheasant 6, 13
green tea 27

H
habitat loss 17
history 36–37
Hokkaido 4, 5, 8, 25
holidays 24
hot springs 8, 12
houses 30

I
invasive species 14
islands 4, 8, 9, 11, 16, 17
isolation 37

J
Japanese black weasel 42, 43
Japanese boars 42
Japanese crested ibis 17
Japanese macaques 12
Japanese serow 13
judo 21

K
kami 22, 24
kanji 31, 33
karate 21
kawaii 20
kiji (green pheasant) 6, 13
kimonos 6, 7, 24
koi carp 6, 14, 24
Korea 9
Kurushima Kaikyō Bridge 4
Kyushu 4, 5, 8

46

L

lotus flowers 16
luck 19

M

macaques 12
maneki-neko 19
manga 20
manners 18
martial arts 21
Meiji Restoration 37
missionaries, Christian 37
mountains 8, 9, 10, 22
Mount Fuji 10–11, 42

N

names 19
New Year's Eve 24
ninjas 36
Nippon 7
Nomura's jellyfish 15

O

Okinawa 4, 5, 8, 9, 17
Okinawa rail 17
Omizutori 25
One-Inch Boy 38–41
onsen 8, 12
origami 19

P

Pacific Ocean 5, 8, 9
pastimes 9, 20–21
plant life 16, 42–43
politeness 18
pop culture 20
population 6, 7

R

raccoon dogs 13
ramen 26
religions 10, 16, 22–23
rice 26, 27, 28, 31, 36

S

sakura (cherry blossom) 6, 16, 25
sandwiches 27, 29
school day diary 32–35
school duties 33
schools 19, 31
Sea of Japan 12
serow 13
Shiba Inu 14
Shikoku 4, 5
Shinto 22
shoguns 37
shrines 22, 24
snapping turtles 14
snow festival 25
snow monkeys 12
spider crabs 15
spirits 22, 24
sports 9, 21
sumo 21
sushi 26, 28

T

tanuki 13
tea ceremony 27, 35
technology 31
temples 23
titles 19
toban 33
Tokyo 5, 6, 7, 10, 20, 26
transportation 5, 7, 37
Tsushima current 12

V

vending machines 6
video games 20
volcanoes 8, 10–11

W

wildlife 9, 12–17, 42–43
work 31
world wars 37

Y

yakusugi 16

ACKNOWLEDGMENTS

The publisher would like to thank the following for their kind permission to reproduce their photographs:

(Key: a-above; b-below/bottom; c-centre; f-far; l-left; r-right; t-top)

Adobe Stock: aomas 24t, kuremo 20cl, norikko 27cl, nata_vkusidey 27clb;
Alamy Stock Photo: cpa media pte ltd / pictures from history 36clb, granger, nyc. 37cra;
Dreamstime.com: volodymyr byrdyak 43cl, matias del carmine 22cra, chernetskaya 29br, cowardlion 6bl, 23clb, jungleoutthere 33cr, kaiskynet 35ca, sergii koval 27cla, kozpho 26tr, roman lupasco 29 (fruits), luciano mortula 37br, rumata7 15clb, sabelskaya 31bc, syda productions 12, wdeon 8, yulianny 29cr; **Getty Images:** the asahi shimbun 25cl;
Shutterstock.com: aratehortua 31cl, baharudin design 27bc, 28tr, bibit padi.Adv 26b, bmc rider 16bl, buttchi 3 sha life 8bl, chaossart 19tl, tyler clemons 14tr, divingraphy 15tl, eqroy 23cla, faber14 9bc, feathercollector 13tr, rika fujita 32b, graphicsn 11tr, jamshed hameed 37cr, hand draw 11clb, hawk777 43cr, ducka_house 27bc (curry), hstrongart 28bl, ikanimo 7t, 23tr, yasuo inoue 13b, miki ishikawa 34b, itzavu 20br, arthit kaeoratanapattama 22, karins 29bl, lyudmyla kharlamova 28-29 (paper x2), kobkul 30b, kohuku 6, kpg-payless 21cl, leungchopan 16cla, wang liqiang 17b, borodacheva marina 32-33, 34-35, maroke 18, 31tl, elizaveta melentyeva 5, metamorworks 7cl, milatas 24bl, guido montaldo 17tl, luciano mortula - lgm 10, new africa 19tr, nishihama 27tl, norinori303 9cl, nussar 25tl, oneinchpunch 30, rui palma 15cl, sean pavone 25bl, photovolcanica.Com 11cla, nicole piepgras 14b, pimnada 35br, anurak pongpatimet 24br, praew stock 16clb, lio putra 21b, sarfaraz82 4, yudi setiyoko 21tr, siro46 19b, souga.Biz 27br, siriwat sriphojaroen 37tr, subakyy 27bl, t-mizuguchi 9tr, keith tarrier 37crb, wulong tommy 17tr, travel mania 36, trialist 13tl, tsuchi 42cr, umarazak 7b, irina vaneeva 14tl, mei yi 16tl, zuestudio 20tr

Cover images: front: **Getty Images:** corbis documentary / andria patino cr, digitalvision / matteo colombo br; getty images / **iStock:** digitalvision vectors / mattjeacock tr, nirut punshiri t; **Shutterstock.com:** vibrands studio bl; back: **Dreamstime.com:** kaiskynet cl; **Shutterstock.com:** nicole piepgras bl, mei yi tl

All of the books in the *Super World* series have been reviewed by authenticity readers of the cultures represented.